Frank Longo & Peter Gordon

An imprint of Sterling Publishing Co., Inc.
www.puzzlewright.com

Puzzlewright Press and the distinctive Puzzlewright Press logo
are trademarks of Sterling Publishing Co., Inc.

2 4 6 8 10 9 7 5 3 1

Published by Sterling Publishing Co., Inc.
387 Park Avenue South, New York, NY 10016

Distributed in Canada by Sterling Publishing
c/o Canadian Manda Group, 165 Dufferin Street,
Toronto, Ontario, Canada M6K 3H6

Manufactured in the United States of America

Sterling ISBN 978-1-4027-6569-8

For information about custom editions, special sales, premium and
corporate purchases, please contact Sterling Special Sales
Department at 800-805-5489 or specialsales@sterlingpublishing.com.

CONTENTS

INTRODUCTION

What do you get when you combine sudoku with SCRABBLE™? Why, this book, of course! In the unlikely event that you haven't yet heard of sudoku, this is a type of logic puzzle that in the past several years has become very popular and has spread like wildfire in magazines, books, and even tabloid newspapers. The appeal of sudoku lies in its simplicity coupled with its addictiveness.

The rules are very simple. You are given a 9×9 grid subdivided into smaller heavily outlined regions. At the start, you are given a few numbers in the grid. Your task is to place a number in each empty cell so that all of the numbers from 1 to 9 appear in each row going across, each column going down, and each heavily outlined region. This is accomplished using logic only, so that the solver should never have to blindly guess. Each puzzle has a unique solution; that is, with the starting numbers given, there is only one possible solution that will work.

Here is an example of a sudoku puzzle and its solution:

9	3	4	7					
2			9					7
	1	6		3				9
					3			
		5	1		2	6		
			6					
8				4		9	6	
4					1			5
					9	1	3	4

9	3	4	7	2	8	5	1	6
2	5	8	9	1	6	3	4	7
7	1	6	5	3	4	8	2	9
6	8	7	4	5	3	2	9	1
3	4	5	1	9	2	6	7	8
1	2	9	6	8	7	4	5	3
8	7	1	3	4	5	9	6	2
4	9	3	2	6	1	7	8	5
5	6	2	8	7	9	1	3	4

Sudoku can be quite addictive. But being crossword lovers, we wanted to add an element of wordplay to the puzzle for variety. So we substituted letters for numbers. This adds some spice to the mix, since every puzzle, while employing the same rules for solving, uses different letters.

Below each grid you are given some letters. These are to be placed into the grid so that all the letters appear in each row, each column, and each of the heavily outlined regions. Now, here's the fun part: when the puzzle is correctly solved, a word will appear somewhere in the grid, either in one of the rows, one of the columns, or on the diagonal from the upper left to the lower right. Here is an example:

V	G	I	R					
E			V					R
	D	O		G				V
					G			
		N	D		E	O		
			O					
U				I		V	O	
I					D			N
					V	D	G	I

V	G	I	R	E	U	N	D	O
E	N	U	V	D	O	G	I	R
R	D	O	N	G	I	U	E	V
O	U	R	I	N	G	E	V	D
G	I	N	D	V	E	O	R	U
D	E	V	O	U	R	I	N	G
U	R	D	G	I	N	V	O	E
I	V	G	E	O	D	R	U	N
N	O	E	U	R	V	D	G	I

G O U R D V I N E

In the solution, the word DEVOURING appears in the sixth row.

Note that the puzzle with letters above is the exact same puzzle as the sudoku puzzle on the previous page, except that the numbers have been replaced by letters. All the 1's became D's, all the 2's became E's, etc. It is solved exactly the same, but with letters instead of numbers. When solving a sudoku puzzle, you are constantly counting to yourself when looking for what numbers are missing. For this reason, we have placed the letters below the grid in an arrangement that's easy to remember, in this case "GOURD VINE." You will say those letters over and over to yourself while solving. As you are solving, you will eventually see a word being formed. Obviously, the knowledge that a word must appear somewhere in the grid can be quite helpful in the solving process. Filling in the missing letters will give you a little more information than you would have had if the puzzle had just contained numbers. You should be warned, though, that just because a word appears to be forming doesn't necessarily make it the correct word. A few traps have been put in the puzzles where near-misses of words are in the solutions. Logic should always trump assumption! Note that at no point is it necessary to identify the word in the grid to logically solve the puzzle. You could speak Serbo-Croatian only, without knowing a word of English, and still logically work your way through each puzzle (though you wouldn't be able to read this introduction).

In this book, we decided to make the puzzles 7×7 cells so that the answer words would all be seven letters. Words of that length are important to know when playing SCRABBLE, since they score a 50-point bonus. All the final answer words in this book are legal words when playing SCRABBLE. The seven letters under the grid are arranged to form either another legitimate seven-letter SCRABBLE word, or two shorter legit words.

Since we chose to use seven-letter words, the grids in this book had to be 7×7 instead of the usual 9×9. This means that instead of 3×3 heavily outlined regions where every letter appears once, there are odd-shaped areas that always have seven cells in them. There are 10 different grid patterns in the book. In every case, fill in the letters so that all the rows, all the columns, and all the heavily outlined regions of seven cells contain each of the letters below the grid exactly once.

The puzzles in this book are arranged by increasing difficulty level, as follows:

1–9: Beginner	43–52: Medium-Hard
10–22: Very Easy	53–62: Hard
23–32: Easy	63–69: Very Hard
33–42: Medium	70–72: Expert

The harder puzzles may require some advanced logic steps and a bit more patience, but ultimately they can be conquered, as previously stated, without having to resort to flat-out guessing. Always bear in mind that every puzzle has a unique solution.

—Frank Longo & Peter Gordon

1

P_3	K_5				C_3	
		U_1				
	I_1		U_1			P_3
		K_5		C_3		
C_3			K_5		D_2	
				N_1		
	U_1				I_1	C_3

P_3	I_1	N_1	K_5	C_3	U_1	D_2

2

J_8					O_1	
		L_1		J_8		
R_1	O_1		F_4			
L_1	J_8				E_1	I_1
			O_1		F_4	R_1
		I_1		O_1		
	L_1					J_8

L_1	I_1	F_4	E_1	R_1	J_8	O_1

3

		C_3			I_1	A_1
				H_4	T_1	
T_1	C_3					
			A_1			
					O_1	B_3
	B_3	I_1				
A_1	H_4			T_1		

C_3	O_1	H_4	A_1	B_3	I_1	T_1

4

D_2		A_1	N_1			
V_4						
K_5	E_1			N_1	D_2	
	D_2				A_1	
	V_4	Y_4			N_1	K_5
						A_1
			V_4	A_1		D_2

V_4	E_1	N_1	D_2	Y_4	A_1	K_5

5

	Q_{10}		L_1	I_1	E_1	
		T_1		Q_{10}		
E_1					A_1	
Q_{10}						U_1
	L_1					I_1
		A_1		E_1		
	E_1	I_1	Q_{10}		U_1	

E_1	Q_{10}	U_1	A_1	L_1	I_1	T_1

6

H_4		T_1	O_1			
				H_4		R_1
	R_1					G_2
W_4						H_4
A_1					R_1	
R_1		A_1				
			H_4	W_4		T_1

G_2 R_1 O_1 W_4 H_4 A_1 T_1

7

		K_5	R_1		E_1	
	K_5			S_1		E_1
F_4						S_1
		E_1		Y_4		
R_1						K_5
K_5		S_1			R_1	
	R_1		Y_4	K_5		

K_5	E_1	Y_4	F_4	U_1	R_1	S_1

8

B_3	W_4					
	H_4		W_4			
		H_4		W_4		B_3
I_1						S_1
H_4		Z_{10}		I_1		
			Z_{10}		B_3	
					Z_{10}	I_1

W_4	H_4	I_1	Z_{10}	S_1	O_1	B_3

9

	A_1	E_1				
	E_1		A_1			
		B_3				A_1
A_1			S_1			B_3
O_1				A_1		
			G_2		S_1	
				B_3	A_1	

B_3	O_1	N_1	E_1	G_2	A_1	S_1

10

	I_1		S_1		R_1	
A_1		M_3				
G_2	A_1					
		S_1		O_1		
					I_1	G_2
				G_2		O_1
	G_2		A_1		S_1	

I_1	S_1	O_1	G_2	R_1	A_1	M_3

11

			T			
W	O	B				
					M	O
		T		O		
I	S					
				W	S	T
			O			

W	O	M	B	S	I	T

12

	U		L		F	
I						
	I		E		B	
	B				U	
	L		F		I	
						B
	F		I		E	

F	O	B	L	I	E	U

13

G_2					E_1	
U_1			B_3			
E_1		A_1				
A_1	B_3				H_4	G_2
				B_3		E_1
			A_1			B_3
	R_1					A_1

H_4 U_1 B_3 R_1 A_1 G_2 E_1

14

						S_1
	K_5	E_1				W_4
B_3	S_1	K_5				
			W_4			
				R_1	K_5	B_3
W_4				E_1	B_3	
E_1						

I_1	R_1	K_5	S_1	W_4	E_1	B_3

15

	Q$_{10}$		U$_{1}$			
		I$_{1}$	Q$_{10}$		B$_{3}$	
T$_{1}$						
Q$_{10}$						T$_{1}$
						Z$_{10}$
	T$_{1}$		Z$_{10}$	I$_{1}$		
			B$_{3}$		T$_{1}$	

Q$_{10}$	U$_{1}$	I$_{1}$	Z$_{10}$	B$_{3}$	E$_{1}$	T$_{1}$

16

	E_1	A_1				
B_3						
	R_1		E_1			G_2
A_1						E_1
G_2			D_2		B_3	
						A_1
				E_1	I_1	

R_1	I_1	D_2	E_1	B_3	A_1	G_2

17

			R_1			
T_1			O_1		R_1	
				A_1		O_1
	X_8				N_1	
N_1		O_1				
	H_4		T_1			R_1
			A_1			

T_1	A_1	X_8	H_4	O_1	R_1	N_1

18

R_1		I_1				
A_1				B_3	L_1	
	B_3					
T_1			A_1			R_1
					R_1	
	G_2	R_1				B_3
				G_2		T_1

T_1	R_1	I_1	G_2	L_1	A_1	B_3

19

					N_1	A_1
I_1	J_8				B_3	
			B_3			J_8
		E_1		A_1		
J_8			S_1			
	S_1				I_1	B_3
B_3	A_1					

S_1	A_1	N_1	E_1	J_8	I_1	B_3

20

K_5		N_1		U_1		
T_1			K_5			
	P_3			K_5		
	N_1				T_1	
		U_1			N_1	
			S_1			U_1
		I_1		T_1		P_3

K_5	N_1	I_1	T_1	S_1	U_1	P_3

21

	T_1					E_1
		P_3			L_1	
Z_{10}					T_1	
	I_1				R_1	
	E_1					T_1
	P_3			I_1		
I_1					P_3	

L_1	I_1	T_1	P_3	R_1	E_1	Z_{10}

22

			A_1			
		S_1			I_1	
U_1				A_1	R_1	
I_1						A_1
	T_1	I_1				U_1
	S_1			T_1		
			S_1			

A_1	T_1	R_1	I_1	U_1	M_3	S_1

23

			H_4			
Y_4			L_1			K_5
		S_1		O_1		
		K_5		S_1		
S_1			O_1			Y_4
			Y_4			

L_1 O_1 C_3 H_4 S_1 K_5 Y_4

24

		H_4			I_1	
				T_1		I_1
	T_1		R_1			
		T_1		M_3		
			S_1		T_1	
S_1		M_3				
	O_1			S_1		

S_1	T_1	I_1	R_1	O_1	H_4	M_3

25

		A$_1$		K$_5$	I$_1$	
N$_1$					K$_5$	F$_4$
F$_4$	K$_5$					R$_1$
	R$_1$	K$_5$		F$_4$		

T$_1$	A$_1$	N$_1$	K$_5$	F$_4$	I$_1$	R$_1$

2 6

			S_1	E_1	H_4	
B_3						
					S_1	
H_4						O_1
	E_1					
						P_3
	U_1	E_1	P_3			

H_4	O_1	S_1	E_1	P_3	U_1	B_3

27

		O_1				
					I_1	
T_1			S_1	L_1		
L_1			T_1			I_1
		V_4	I_1			O_1
	L_1					
				T_1		

L_1	O_1	V_4	E_1	S_1	I_1	T_1

28

	I_1		R_1			
			C_3		I_1	
	M_3					O_1
O_1					M_3	
	R_1		M_3			
			S_1		O_1	

C_3	O_1	N_1	S_1	R_1	I_1	M_3

29

					S_1	N_1
S_1					F_4	
	L_1	S_1		E_1		
		N_1		G_2	L_1	
	G_2					L_1
F_4	E_1					

F_4	L_1	A_1	N_1	G_2	E_1	S_1

30

					K_5	
T_1			H_4	C_3		
H_4			E_1		C_3	
	H_4		P_3			U_1
		H_4	K_5			T_1
	U_1					

H_4	U_1	T_1	P_3	E_1	C_3	K_5

31

A_1		E_1				
	N_1			H_4		
G_2	O_1					E_1
O_1					H_4	X_8
		N_1			A_1	
				X_8		H_4

O_1	X_8	E_1	N_1	H_4	A_1	G_2

32

E_1			Y_4			A_1
					H_4	
	H_4				E_1	W_4
H_4	A_1				W_4	
	Y_4					
A_1			R_1			H_4

Y_4	E_1	W_4	H_4	A_1	I_1	R_1

33

	A_1				N_1	L_1
			A_1			
	D_2					
		I_1		L_1		
					A_1	
			S_1			
I_1	L_1				R_1	

L_1	A_1	R_1	D_2	S_1	I_1	N_1

34

		I_1	A_1	U_1		
					C_3	
			H_4			
	A_1				I_1	
			I_1			
	F_4					
		U_1	C_3	I_1		

H_4	A_1	F_4	I_1	C_3	U_1	S_1

35

	K_5			Y_4		
				R_1		
	J_8		C_3		Y_4	
	R_1		Y_4		O_1	
		A_1				
		J_8			R_1	

J_8	O_1	Y_4	R_1	A_1	C_3	K_5

36

						R_1
R_1		C_3			Z_{10}	S_1
		Z_{10}		S_1		
T_1	C_3			R_1		A_1
I_1						

C_3	A_1	R_1	Z_{10}	I_1	T_1	S_1

37

				L_1		
				N_1		R_1
				E_1	P_3	
	P_3				R_1	
	A_1	L_1				
A_1		R_1				
		P_3				

I_1	N_1	P_3	E_1	A_1	R_1	L_1

38

	A_1					N_1
					C_3	
		W_4			S_1	
		A_1		P_3		
	C_3			O_1		
	N_1					
C_3					A_1	

S_1 N_1 O_1 W_4 C_3 A_1 P_3

39

S			N		E	
					U	
		P				
	U				N	
				U		
	P					
	K		S			U

S P E L U N K

40

					F_4	E_1
					W_4	
					L_1	
E_1			A_1			P_3
	O_1					
	A_1					
O_1	F_4					

W_4	O_1	L_1	F_4	A_1	P_3	E_1

41

S_1		U_1	R_1			
		S_1	M_3			
			B_3			
			H_4	M_3		
			S_1	R_1		B_3

M_3	O_1	S_1	H_4	R_1	U_1	B_3

42

C_3						A_1
	H_4	W_4		O_1		
	L_1				A_1	
		A_1		C_3	L_1	
H_4						S_1

O_1	W_4	L_1	C_3	A_1	S_1	H_4

4 3

						I
A		E				L
	M				R	
	R				L	
	L				N	
L				M		N
M						

M	A	R	L	I	N	E

44

			I_1		T_1	
T_1			N_1			I_1
	B_3					N_1
B_3					D_2	
I_1			B_3			A_1
	G_2		D_2			

G_2	N_1	A_1	T_1	B_3	I_1	D_2

45

N_1			C_3		F_4	
		D_2				R_1
		F_4		O_1		
F_4				D_2		
	N_1		E_1			F_4

F_4	E_1	R_1	N_1	D_2	O_1	C_3

46

	A_1		X_8			
	O_1				A_1	
X_8					I_1	
	X_8					A_1
	T_1				E_1	
			E_1		T_1	

C_3	O_1	A_1	X_8	T_1	I_1	E_1

47

		O				
	I	A				
			P	O		
		R	T			
				I	A	
				A		

A P R I C O T

48

	V_4		G_2			U_1
A_1		S_1				
				R_1		E_1
E_1			U_1		A_1	

V_4 A_1 S_1 E_1 R_1 U_1 G_2

49

F_4					A_1	
		A_1				
			S_1			U_1
		T_1		F_4		
U_1			T_1			
				O_1		
	U_1					O_1

O_1	A_1	F_4	S_1	M_3	U_1	T_1

50

		O_1	B_3	E_1		
N_1						
E_1		A_1		W_4		J_8
						W_4
		W_4	O_1	B_3		

J_8	A_1	W_4	B_3	O_1	N_1	E_1

51

			A			
R			T			
				E		
		R		T		
		S				
			N			E
			R			

T_1 R_1 E_1 P_3 A_1 N_1 S_1

52

		E				
			L			C
C					O	
		T		P		
	E					O
T			O			
				T		

T	O	P	C	L	U	E

53

	O_1	A_1		H_4		
		H_4			E_1	
		E_1	O_1	C_3		
	A_1			O_1		
		R_1		E_1	H_4	

H_4	E_1	R_1	C_3	O_1	L_1	A_1

54

E_1		I_1				
B_3			U_1			R_1
		U_1				
			G_2			
				U_1		
R_1			E_1			I_1
				I_1		B_3

F_4	U_1	R_1	G_2	I_1	B_3	E_1

55

				T_1	H_4	
	L_1	Z_{10}			M_3	
L_1						A_1
	M_3			A_1	Z_{10}	
	S_1	A_1				

S_1	H_4	M_3	A_1	L_1	T_1	Z_{10}

56

R_1		K_5	E_1			
				D_2		C_3
			K_5			
D_2		R_1				
			D_2	K_5		Y_4

D_2	R_1	Y_4	C_3	A_1	K_5	E_1

57

L_1		I_1				
R_1				M_3	L_1	
			E_1			
	M_3	N_1				R_1
				I_1		K_5

R_1	I_1	N_1	K_5	E_1	L_1	M_3

5 8

	L_1					
O_1						T_1
I_1						B_3
	O_1				I_1	
N_1						K_5
T_1						I_1
					N_1	

T_1	O_1	B_3	L_1	I_1	N_1	K_5

59

				L		
		T				
			B	R	S	
		S		E		
	T	I	L			
				T		
		B				

B L I S T E R

60

		C_3				
		K_5		I_1		
	M_3		C_3			
	U_1				S_1	
			I_1		T_1	
		M_3		K_5		
				C_3		

S_1 K_5 I_1 M_3 C_3 U_1 T_1

61

			C_3			
P_3		C_3				
						E_1
S_1						P_3
E_1						
				L_1		A_1
			L_1			

S_1	P_3	E_1	C_3	L_1	A_1	G_2

6 2

	Y_4			P_3		
P_3		A_1	R_1		F_4	
	P_3		F_4	Y_4		R_1
		T_1			L_1	

R_1	A_1	F_4	T_1	P_3	L_1	Y_4

63

			L_1			
				W_4		
	T_1		E_1	L_1	O_1	
	W_4	E_1	B_3		T_1	
		T_1				
			A_1			

A_1	T_1	B_3	E_1	L_1	O_1	W_4

64

				F_4		
				L_1		D_2
L_1	I_1					
					T_1	E_1
Y_4		I_1				
		L_1				

F_4	E_1	T_1	I_1	D_2	L_1	Y_4

65

	S_1	F_4	A_1			
A_1		L_1				
			M_3			
				O_1		F_4
			F_4	T_1	S_1	

S_1 L_1 A_1 M_3 O_1 F_4 T_1

66

	A_{1}				E_{1}	
			A_{1}	Z_{10}	F_{4}	
	Z_{10}	P_{3}	E_{1}			
	E_{1}				N_{1}	

F_{4}	A_{1}	Z_{10}	E_{1}	P_{3}	I_{1}	N_{1}

67

	S_1		O_1		E_1	
F_4						S_1
			E_1			
O_1						T_1
	R_1		W_4		F_4	

S_1	E_1	W_4	F_4	O_1	R_1	T_1

68

				I_1		
		A_1		W_4		
						G_2
G_2			P_3			W_4
E_1						
		W_4		B_3		
		P_3				

B_3 A_1 G_2 W_4 I_1 P_3 E_1

69

			M_3	E_1		
				T_1		P_3
			K_5			
E_1		N_1				
		T_1	U_1			

M_3 E_1 T_1 P_3 U_1 N_1 K_5

70

A			S			
						U
G			U			
			A			
			H			G
U						
			E			H

S H A G E M U

71

		R		N		
E		M				
A						R
				O		I
		E		A		

R O M A I N E

72

U_1			G_2			
G_2						T_1
P_3						O_1
O_1						G_2
			T_1			L_1

T_1	O_1	E_1	P_3	L_1	U_1	G_2

ANSWERS

1

P	K	D	I	U	C	N
D	C	U	P	K	N	I
N	I	C	U	D	K	P
I	P	K	N	C	U	D
C	N	P	K	I	D	U
U	D	I	C	N	P	K
K	U	N	D	P	I	C

2

J	I	R	L	E	O	F
E	F	L	I	J	R	O
R	O	E	F	I	J	L
L	J	O	R	F	E	I
I	E	J	O	L	F	R
F	R	I	J	O	L	E
O	L	F	E	R	I	J

3

H	O	C	T	B	I	A
B	I	A	O	H	T	C
T	C	B	I	O	A	H
C	T	H	A	I	B	O
I	A	T	H	C	O	B
O	B	I	C	A	H	T
A	H	O	B	T	C	I

4

D	Y	A	N	K	E	V
V	A	N	D	Y	K	E
K	E	V	A	N	D	Y
Y	D	E	K	V	A	N
A	V	Y	E	D	N	K
N	K	D	Y	E	V	A
E	N	K	V	A	Y	D

5

A	Q	U	L	I	E	T
L	U	T	A	Q	I	E
E	I	L	T	U	A	Q
Q	A	E	I	T	L	U
U	L	Q	E	A	T	I
I	T	A	U	E	Q	L
T	E	I	Q	L	U	A

6

H	W	T	O	R	G	A
G	A	O	W	H	T	R
T	R	H	A	O	W	G
W	T	G	R	A	O	H
A	H	W	G	T	R	O
R	O	A	T	G	H	W
O	G	R	H	W	A	T

7

S	U	K	R	F	E	Y
Y	K	R	U	S	F	E
F	E	Y	K	R	U	S
U	F	E	S	Y	K	R
R	S	F	E	U	Y	K
K	Y	S	F	E	R	U
E	R	U	Y	K	S	F

8

B	W	S	I	Z	H	O
S	H	O	W	B	I	Z
Z	I	H	S	W	O	B
I	Z	B	O	H	W	S
H	O	Z	B	I	S	W
W	S	I	Z	O	B	H
O	B	W	H	S	Z	I

9

G	A	E	B	S	O	N
B	E	O	A	G	N	S
S	N	B	O	E	G	A
A	G	N	S	O	E	B
O	S	G	N	A	B	E
E	B	A	G	N	S	O
N	O	S	E	B	A	G

10

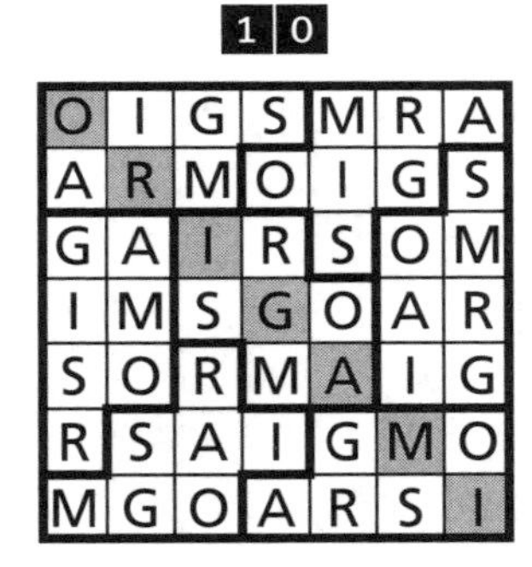

O	I	G	S	M	R	A
A	R	M	O	I	G	S
G	A	I	R	S	O	M
I	M	S	G	O	A	R
S	O	R	M	A	I	G
R	S	A	I	G	M	O
M	G	O	A	R	S	I

11

M	I	S	T	B	O	W
W	O	B	M	T	I	S
T	W	I	B	S	M	O
B	M	T	S	O	W	I
I	S	O	W	M	T	B
O	B	M	I	W	S	T
S	T	W	O	I	B	M

12

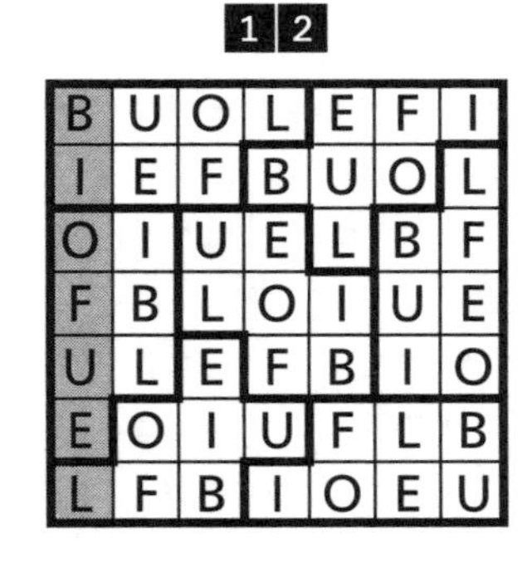

B	U	O	L	E	F	I
I	E	F	B	U	O	L
O	I	U	E	L	B	F
F	B	L	O	I	U	E
U	L	E	F	B	I	O
E	O	I	U	F	L	B
L	F	B	I	O	E	U

13

G	A	B	R	U	E	H
U	H	E	B	A	G	R
E	G	A	H	R	B	U
A	B	R	U	E	H	G
R	U	H	G	B	A	E
H	E	U	A	G	R	B
B	R	G	E	H	U	A

14

R	W	I	B	K	E	S
S	K	E	R	B	I	W
B	S	K	E	W	R	I
K	R	B	W	I	S	E
I	E	W	S	R	K	B
W	I	S	K	E	B	R
E	B	R	I	S	W	K

15

B	Q	T	U	E	Z	I
Z	E	I	Q	T	B	U
T	I	Z	E	U	Q	B
Q	Z	U	I	B	E	T
U	B	E	T	Q	I	Z
E	T	B	Z	I	U	Q
I	U	Q	B	Z	T	E

16

I	E	A	R	B	G	D
B	D	G	A	R	E	I
D	R	B	E	I	A	G
A	B	R	I	G	D	E
G	I	E	D	A	B	R
E	G	I	B	D	R	A
R	A	D	G	E	I	B

17

A	O	X	R	H	T	N
T	N	A	O	X	R	H
H	R	T	N	A	X	O
O	X	R	H	T	N	A
N	A	O	X	R	H	T
X	H	N	T	O	A	R
R	T	H	A	N	O	X

18

R	L	I	T	A	B	G
A	T	G	R	B	L	I
G	B	L	I	R	T	A
T	I	B	A	L	G	R
B	A	T	G	I	R	L
I	G	R	L	T	A	B
L	R	A	B	G	I	T

19

S	E	B	I	J	N	A
I	J	A	N	E	B	S
A	N	S	B	I	E	J
N	B	E	J	A	S	I
J	I	N	S	B	A	E
E	S	J	A	N	I	B
B	A	I	E	S	J	N

20

K	I	N	P	U	S	T
T	U	S	K	I	P	N
S	P	T	N	K	U	I
U	N	P	I	S	T	K
I	K	U	T	P	N	S
P	T	K	S	N	I	U
N	S	I	U	T	K	P

21

P	T	I	R	L	Z	E
E	R	P	Z	T	L	I
Z	L	E	I	P	T	R
L	I	Z	T	E	R	P
R	E	L	P	Z	I	T
T	P	R	L	I	E	Z
I	Z	T	E	R	P	L

22

S	M	R	A	I	U	T
T	A	S	R	U	I	M
U	I	M	T	A	R	S
I	R	T	U	S	M	A
A	T	I	M	R	S	U
M	S	U	I	T	A	R
R	U	A	S	M	T	I

23

O	K	C	H	Y	S	L
Y	S	O	L	C	H	K
H	L	S	K	O	Y	C
K	C	Y	S	H	L	O
L	Y	K	C	S	O	H
S	H	L	O	K	C	Y
C	O	H	Y	L	K	S

24

T	S	H	M	O	I	R
M	R	O	H	T	S	I
I	T	S	R	H	O	M
R	I	T	O	M	H	S
O	M	I	S	R	T	H
S	H	M	T	I	R	O
H	O	R	I	S	M	T

25

K	I	R	T	N	F	A
T	F	A	R	K	I	N
N	T	I	A	R	K	F
A	N	F	K	T	R	I
F	K	N	I	A	T	R
I	R	K	N	F	A	T
R	A	T	F	I	N	K

26

P	O	U	S	E	H	B
B	H	S	U	P	O	E
E	P	O	B	U	S	H
H	B	P	E	S	U	O
S	E	H	O	B	P	U
U	S	B	H	O	E	P
O	U	E	P	H	B	S

27

V	I	O	L	E	T	S
S	E	L	O	V	I	T
T	V	I	S	L	O	E
L	S	E	T	O	V	I
E	T	V	I	S	L	O
O	L	T	E	I	S	V
I	O	S	V	T	E	L

28

M	I	C	R	O	S	N
N	O	R	C	M	I	S
S	M	I	N	R	C	O
C	S	M	O	N	R	I
O	N	S	I	C	M	R
I	R	O	M	S	N	C
R	C	N	S	I	O	M

29

L	F	G	E	A	S	N
S	A	E	L	N	F	G
N	L	S	G	E	A	F
G	N	F	A	L	E	S
A	S	N	F	G	L	E
E	G	A	S	F	N	L
F	E	L	N	S	G	A

30

E	P	C	U	T	K	H
T	K	U	H	C	P	E
H	T	P	E	U	C	K
K	E	T	C	H	U	P
C	H	K	P	E	T	U
U	C	H	K	P	E	T
P	U	E	T	K	H	C

31

A	G	E	H	O	X	N
X	N	O	E	H	G	A
G	O	H	X	A	N	E
N	H	X	A	G	E	O
O	E	A	G	N	H	X
H	X	N	O	E	A	G
E	A	G	N	X	O	H

32

E	W	H	Y	I	R	A
I	R	A	W	Y	H	E
R	H	Y	I	A	E	W
Y	E	W	A	H	I	R
H	A	I	E	R	W	Y
W	Y	R	H	E	A	I
A	I	E	R	W	Y	H

33

D	A	S	R	I	N	L
L	I	N	A	R	S	D
N	D	R	L	S	I	A
A	S	I	N	L	D	R
S	R	L	I	D	A	N
R	N	D	S	A	L	I
I	L	A	D	N	R	S

34

F	C	I	A	U	S	H
U	S	H	F	A	C	I
C	I	A	H	S	U	F
H	A	S	U	F	I	C
S	U	F	I	C	H	A
I	F	C	S	H	A	U
A	H	U	C	I	F	S

35

C	K	O	R	Y	J	A
J	A	Y	O	R	K	C
A	J	R	C	K	Y	O
O	Y	K	J	C	A	R
K	R	C	Y	A	O	J
R	O	A	K	J	C	Y
Y	C	J	A	O	R	K

36

S	R	T	C	Z	A	I
Z	A	I	S	C	T	R
R	I	C	A	T	Z	S
A	T	Z	I	S	R	C
T	C	S	Z	R	I	A
I	S	R	T	A	C	Z
C	Z	A	R	I	S	T

37

R	E	A	N	L	I	P
P	L	I	A	N	E	R
I	R	N	L	E	P	A
N	P	E	I	A	R	L
E	A	L	P	R	N	I
A	I	R	E	P	L	N
L	N	P	R	I	A	E

38

P	A	C	S	W	O	N
W	O	N	A	S	C	P
N	P	W	O	C	S	A
O	S	A	W	P	N	C
A	C	S	N	O	P	W
S	N	P	C	A	W	O
C	W	O	P	N	A	S

39

S	L	U	N	K	E	P
P	E	K	L	N	U	S
K	N	P	U	E	S	L
E	U	L	P	S	N	K
L	S	N	K	U	P	E
U	P	S	E	L	K	N
N	K	E	S	P	L	U

40

A	W	O	L	P	F	E
P	E	A	F	O	W	L
F	P	W	O	E	L	A
E	L	F	A	W	O	P
W	O	L	P	A	E	F
L	A	E	W	F	P	O
O	F	P	E	L	A	W

41

M	R	B	O	H	S	U
S	H	U	R	B	M	O
H	O	S	M	U	B	R
U	M	R	B	S	O	H
R	B	O	H	M	U	S
O	U	M	S	R	H	B
B	S	H	U	O	R	M

42

C	W	H	S	L	O	A
L	C	O	A	S	H	W
A	H	W	L	O	S	C
O	L	S	C	W	A	H
W	S	A	H	C	L	O
S	A	C	O	H	W	L
H	O	L	W	A	C	S

43

R	E	L	M	N	A	I
A	N	E	I	R	M	L
I	M	A	N	L	R	E
N	R	I	E	A	L	M
E	L	M	R	I	N	A
L	I	R	A	M	E	N
M	A	N	L	E	I	R

44

N	A	B	I	G	T	D
T	D	G	N	A	B	I
G	B	A	T	D	I	N
D	I	N	G	B	A	T
B	T	I	A	N	D	G
I	N	D	B	T	G	A
A	G	T	D	I	N	B

45

N	D	E	C	R	F	O
E	F	D	O	N	C	R
O	R	N	F	E	D	C
R	C	F	D	O	N	E
C	O	R	N	F	E	D
F	E	C	R	D	O	N
D	N	O	E	C	R	F

46

I	A	O	X	E	C	T
T	O	C	I	X	A	E
X	E	T	A	O	I	C
E	I	A	C	T	X	O
C	X	E	T	I	O	A
A	T	I	O	C	E	X
O	C	X	E	A	T	I

47

P	T	O	I	R	C	A
O	I	A	C	T	R	P
A	R	T	P	O	I	C
R	P	I	A	C	T	O
C	A	R	T	P	O	I
T	C	P	O	I	A	R
I	O	C	R	A	P	T

48

S	E	V	R	U	G	A
R	V	A	G	S	E	U
A	U	S	E	V	R	G
U	R	G	A	E	V	S
G	A	U	V	R	S	E
E	S	R	U	G	A	V
V	G	E	S	A	U	R

49

F	M	U	O	T	A	S
S	T	A	M	U	O	F
A	O	F	S	M	T	U
O	S	T	A	F	U	M
U	F	O	T	S	M	A
M	A	S	U	O	F	T
T	U	M	F	A	S	O

50

W	J	O	B	E	N	A
N	A	J	W	O	E	B
B	E	N	A	J	W	O
E	B	A	N	W	O	J
O	W	B	E	A	J	N
A	O	E	J	N	B	W
J	N	W	O	B	A	E

51

S	E	N	A	R	P	T
R	P	E	T	N	A	S
T	A	P	S	E	R	N
N	S	R	P	T	E	A
A	T	S	E	P	N	R
P	R	A	N	S	T	E
E	N	T	R	A	S	P

52

U	O	E	T	C	L	P
E	T	P	L	O	U	C
C	P	L	E	U	O	T
O	C	T	U	P	E	L
P	E	U	C	L	T	O
T	L	C	O	E	P	U
L	U	O	P	T	C	E

53

L	O	A	E	H	R	C
R	E	C	A	L	O	H
A	C	H	L	R	E	O
H	R	E	O	C	A	L
E	A	L	H	O	C	R
C	H	O	R	A	L	E
O	L	R	C	E	H	A

54

E	F	I	B	R	U	G
B	I	F	U	G	E	R
G	R	U	I	E	B	F
F	E	R	G	B	I	U
I	B	G	F	U	R	E
R	U	B	E	F	G	I
U	G	E	R	I	F	B

55

H	T	M	Z	S	A	L
M	A	L	S	T	H	Z
S	L	Z	A	H	M	T
L	H	T	M	Z	S	A
T	M	S	L	A	Z	H
Z	S	A	H	L	T	M
A	Z	H	T	M	L	S

56

R	D	K	E	Y	C	A
C	K	A	Y	R	D	E
Y	A	E	R	D	K	C
A	C	D	K	E	Y	R
D	Y	R	A	C	E	K
K	E	Y	C	A	R	D
E	R	C	D	K	A	Y

57

L	K	I	N	E	R	M
R	N	K	I	M	L	E
E	I	M	K	R	N	L
M	L	R	E	N	K	I
K	R	E	M	L	I	N
I	M	N	L	K	E	R
N	E	L	R	I	M	K

58

B	L	O	T	I	K	N
O	K	B	I	N	L	T
I	T	N	L	K	O	B
K	O	T	N	B	I	L
N	B	I	O	L	T	K
T	N	L	K	O	B	I
L	I	K	B	T	N	O

59

T	E	R	S	L	I	B
R	S	T	I	B	L	E
I	L	E	B	R	S	T
B	I	S	T	E	R	L
E	T	I	L	S	B	R
S	B	L	R	T	E	I
L	R	B	E	I	T	S

60

S	K	C	M	T	I	U
T	S	K	U	I	M	C
I	M	U	C	S	K	T
C	U	T	K	M	S	I
K	C	S	I	U	T	M
U	I	M	T	K	C	S
M	T	I	S	C	U	K

61

L	G	P	C	E	A	S
P	E	C	A	S	G	L
A	L	G	S	P	C	E
S	C	A	E	G	L	P
E	A	L	P	C	S	G
C	P	S	G	L	E	A
G	S	E	L	A	P	C

62

L	Y	F	A	P	R	T
F	L	Y	T	R	A	P
P	T	A	R	L	F	Y
R	A	P	L	T	Y	F
A	P	L	F	Y	T	R
T	F	R	Y	A	P	L
Y	R	T	P	F	L	A

63

B	E	A	L	O	W	T
O	A	L	T	W	B	E
W	T	B	E	L	O	A
E	L	O	W	T	A	B
L	W	E	B	A	T	O
A	B	T	O	E	L	W
T	O	W	A	B	E	L

64

E	D	Y	T	F	L	I
T	Y	F	I	L	E	D
L	I	E	D	T	Y	F
D	F	T	L	E	I	Y
F	L	D	Y	I	T	E
Y	T	I	E	D	F	L
I	E	L	F	Y	D	T

65

F	L	O	T	S	A	M
T	S	F	A	M	L	O
A	M	L	O	F	T	S
O	T	S	M	A	F	L
S	A	T	L	O	M	F
L	O	M	F	T	S	A
M	F	A	S	L	O	T

66

F	P	A	N	E	Z	I
Z	A	I	F	P	E	N
E	I	N	A	Z	F	P
P	N	E	Z	F	I	A
N	Z	P	E	I	A	F
I	E	F	P	A	N	Z
A	F	Z	I	N	P	E

67

R	S	T	O	F	E	W
F	O	W	R	E	T	S
E	W	O	S	T	R	F
W	T	F	E	R	S	O
S	F	E	T	W	O	R
O	E	R	F	S	W	T
T	R	S	W	O	F	E

68

W	G	E	B	I	P	A
P	E	A	G	W	I	B
I	A	B	W	P	E	G
G	B	I	P	E	A	W
E	W	G	I	A	B	P
A	P	W	E	B	G	I
B	I	P	A	G	W	E

69

P	T	U	M	E	K	N
N	M	E	P	K	T	U
K	U	M	N	T	E	P
T	E	P	K	N	U	M
E	P	N	T	U	M	K
U	N	K	E	M	P	T
M	K	T	U	P	N	E

70

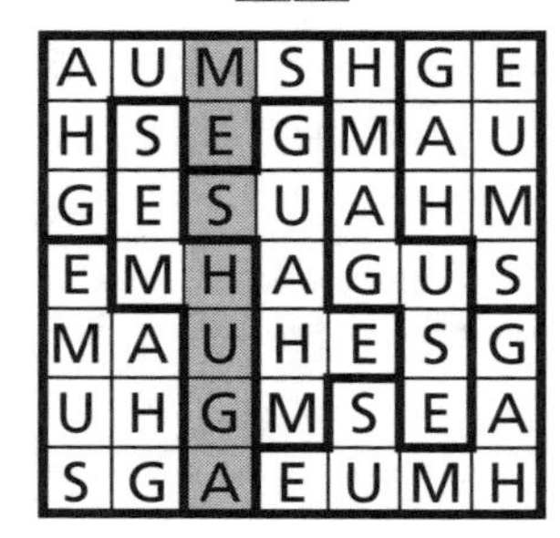

A	U	M	S	H	G	E
H	S	E	G	M	A	U
G	E	S	U	A	H	M
E	M	H	A	G	U	S
M	A	U	H	E	S	G
U	H	G	M	S	E	A
S	G	A	E	U	M	H

71

I	A	R	O	N	E	M
E	R	M	A	I	N	O
N	M	O	E	R	I	A
A	O	I	N	E	M	R
R	N	A	I	M	O	E
M	E	N	R	O	A	I
O	I	E	M	A	R	N

72

T	P	L	O	U	G	E
U	O	E	G	T	L	P
G	E	O	P	L	U	T
P	L	T	U	G	E	O
O	T	U	L	E	P	G
E	U	G	T	P	O	L
L	G	P	E	O	T	U

ALSO AVAILABLE

ABOUT THE AUTHORS

FRANK LONGO and PETER GORDON are the authors of *Mensa® Guide to Solving Sudoku* and *Scrabble-doku*.

Longo has written more than 70 puzzle books, including more than five dozen sudoku books. Some of his titles are *The Big Book of Wordoku Puzzles*, *Cranium-Crushing Crosswords*, *Movie-doku*, *Oy Vey! Sudoku*, *SCRABBLE™ Crosswords*, *Sit & Solve® Wordoku*, *Sports-doku*, *TRIVIAL PURSUIT™ Sudoku*, *The 25-Foot-Long Crossword Puzzle*, and *The World's Longest Sudoku Puzzle*.

Gordon, who was the crossword editor of *The New York Sun*, is the author of several puzzle books, *YAHTZEE Scratch & Play to Go!* being the latest. He writes a current events crossword for *The Week* magazine and he is the proud owner of a vanity license plate that says SUDOKU.